You
Are
Beautiful

Written By : Jessica Heins
Illustrated By : Pinki Basak

This book is inspired by my 3 beautiful daughters Breyanna, Kourtney, and Sharlotte. I am so thankful I have you to love every day. The days are not always easy but with love, joy, laughter,connection and positivity we become stronger, happier, and most of all kinder to others, more importantly, ourselves. With love, Mom

You are BEAUTIFUL…
You are BEAUTIFUL, here's how we know…
Say it 1 time and then again until you feel it in your soul!

I am BEAUTIFUL
I am BEAUTIFUL
Just the way I am!

I am BEAUTIFUL
I am BEAUTIFUL
YES, I AM!

Say it fast, say it s l o w
I am BEAUTIFUL
I am B E A U T I F U L
Just the way I am!

I am BEAUTIFUL
I am BEAUTIFUL
YES, I AM!

Say it quiet, say it LOUD
I am beautiful
I AM BEAUTIFUL
Just the way I am!

I am beautiful
I AM BEAUTIFUL
YES, I AM!

Say it with a smile and feel your beauty grow
I am BEAUTIFUL
I am BEAUTIFUL
Just the way I am!

I am BEAUTIFUL
I am BEAUTIFUL
YES, I AM!

Say it while you sit and say it
when you stand
I am BEAUTIFUL
I am BEAUTIFUL
Just the way I am!

I am BEAUTIFUL
I am BEAUTIFUL
YES, I AM!

Say it with your eyes closed
I am BEAUTIFUL
I am BEAUTIFUL
Just the way I am!

I am BEAUTIFUL
I am BEAUTIFUL
YES, I AM!

Now say it with your heart, really feel it in your soul

I am BEAUTIFUL

I am BEAUTIFUL

Just the way I am!

I am BEAUTIFUL
I am BEAUTIFUL
YES, I AM!

"Beauty" starts with embracing and celebrating the beauty in each individual. It's crucial to recognize that true beauty comes from within and is reflected in the qualities that make us who we are. Kindness, compassion, and love are the qualities that create a lasting impact on the world and those around us.

By appreciating and accepting ourselves and others for our unique qualities, we promote inclusivity and understanding, fostering a more harmonious and beautiful world. Small acts of kindness and expressions of love can create significant positive change, touching the lives of those we encounter.

Let's continue to spread kindness, embrace diversity,
and appreciate the beauty in every person we meet.
Together, we can make the world a more
compassionate and beautiful place for everyone.

THANK YOU!